WIND
IN A BOX

Also by Terrance Hayes

Hip Logic

Muscular Music

WIND
IN A BOX

Terrance Hayes

 PENGUIN POETS

PENGUIN BOOKS

Published by the Penguin Group

Penguin Group (USA) Inc., 375 Hudson Street, New York, New York 10014, U.S.A.

Penguin Group (Canada), 90 Eglinton Avenue East, Suite 700, Toronto, Ontario, Canada M4P 2Y3

(a division of Pearson Penguin Canada Inc.)

Penguin Books Ltd, 80 Strand, London WC2R 0RL, England

Penguin Ireland, 25 St Stephen's Green, Dublin 2, Ireland (a division of Penguin Books Ltd)

Penguin Group (Australia), 250 Camberwell Road, Camberwell, Victoria 3124, Australia

(a division of Pearson Australia Group Pty Ltd)

Penguin Books India Pvt Ltd, 11 Community Centre, Panchsheel Park, New Delhi - 110 017, India

Penguin Group (NZ), cnr Airborne and Rosedale Roads, Albany, Auckland 1310, New Zealand

(a division of Pearson New Zealand Ltd)

Penguin Books (South Africa) (Pty) Ltd, 24 Sturdee Avenue, Rosebank, Johannesburg 2196,South Africa

Penguin Books Ltd, Registered Offices:
80 Strand, London WC2R 0RL, England

First published in Penguin Books 2006

10 9 8 7 6

Copyright © Terrance Hayes, 2006
All rights reserved

Page vii constitutes an extension of this copyright page.

LIBRARY OF CONGRESS CATALOGING IN PUBLICATION DATA
Hayes, Terrance.
Wind in a Box / Terrance Hayes.
p. cm.—(Penguin Poets)
ISBN 978-0-14-303686-9
1. African Americans—Poetry. I. Title.

PS3558.A8378W56 2006
811'. 5—dc22 2005053460

Printed in the United States of America
Set in Helvetica Neue
Designed by Ginger Legato

For Yona and Ua;
and for Aaron becoming

ACKNOWLEDGMENTS

Sincere thanks to the editors and staff of the following publications for first acknowledging the poems (and previous versions of the poems) in this book:

Antioch Review, Ascent, Bay City Review, Black Renaissance Noir, Black Warrior Review, Brilliant Corners, Caketrain, Callaloo, Crowd, 88, failbetter, Fence, Fugue, The Gingko Tree Review, Gulf Coast, Hunger Mountain, The Indiana Review, The Journal, jubilat, The Kenyon Review, Kestral, Pleiades, Ploughshares, Poetry Daily, Swink, Third Coast, Tin House, and *West Branch.*

"The Blue Terrance" [I come from a long line . . ."], "A Postcard from Okemah," "Talk," and "Wind in a Box" ["I claim in the last hour . . ."] also appeared in *Legitimate Dangers: American Poets of the New Century,* Cate Marvin and Michael Dumanis, editors. "Harryette Mullen Lecture on the American Dream" also appeared in *Red, White, and Blues: Poets on the Promise of America,* Virgil Suarez and Ryan G. Van Cleave, editors. "Pine" also appeared in *Gathering Ground: A Reader Celebrating Cave Canem's First Decade,* Toi Derricotte and Cornelius Eady, editors, Camille T. Dungy, assistant editor. "Pine" and "The Whale" also appeared in the *Autumn House Anthology of Contemporary American Poetry,* Sue Ellen Thompson, editor. "Threshold" also appeared in *Poets on Place: Tales and Interviews from the Road,* W. T. Pfefferle, editor. "Tour Daufuskie" also appeared in *The Pushcart Prize XXVIII: Best of Small Presses, 2004,* Bill Henderson, editor. "Variation on a Black Cinema Treasure: Broken Earth" and "Variation on a Black Cinema Treasure: Boogie Woogie Blues" also appeared in the *2005 Best American Poetry,* Paul Muldoon and David Lehman, editors.

Deepest gratitude to Yona Harvey, Tony Hoagland, and Shara McCallum for offering their insights and talents to the completion of this collection; and to the National Endowment for the Arts for its generous support. Thanks, as well, to those who influenced this manuscript through friendship and spirit: Elizabeth Alexander, Radiclani Clytus, the Cave Canem family, Jim Daniels and the CMU community, Joel Dias Porter (DJ Renegade), Paul Slovak, Jeff Thomson, Crystal Williams, and the rest of my kin, both literal and figurative.

CONTENTS

I tell a story of bodies that change . . .
—Ovid's *Metamorphoses* (via DJ Spooky)

(I am large, I contain multitudes.)
—Walt Whitman, "Song of Myself"

WIND
IN A BOX

WIND IN A BOX

This ink. This name. This blood. This blunder.
This blood. This loss. This lonesome wind. This canyon.
This / twin / swiftly / paddling / shadow blooming
an inch above the carpet—. This cry. This mud.
This shudder. This is where I stood: by the bed,
by the door, by the window, in the night / in the night.
How deep, how often / must a woman be touched?
How deep, how often have I been touched?
On the bone, on the shoulder, on the brow, on the knuckle:
Touch like a last name, touch like a wet match.
Touch like an empty shoe and an empty shoe, sweet
and incomprehensible. This ink. This name. This blood
and wonder. This box. This body in a box. This blood
in the body. This wind in the blood.

WOOFER (WHEN I CONSIDER THE AFRICAN-AMERICAN)

When I consider the much discussed dilemma
of the African-American, I think not of the diasporic
middle passing, unchained, juke, jock, and jiving
sons and daughters of what sleek dashikied poets
and tether fisted Nationalists commonly call Mother
Africa, but of an ex-girlfriend who was the child
of a black-skinned Ghanaian beauty and Jewish-
American, globetrotting ethnomusicologist.
I forgot all my father's warnings about meeting women
at bus stops (which is the way he met my mother)
when I met her waiting for the rush hour bus in October
because I have always been a sucker for deep blue denim
and Afros and because she spoke so slowly
when she asked the time. I wrote my phone number
in the back of the book of poems I had and said
something like "You can return it when I see you again"
which has to be one of my top two or three best
pickup lines ever. If you have ever gotten lucky
on a first date you can guess what followed: her smile
twizzling above a tight black v-neck sweater, chatter
on my velvet couch and then the two of us wearing nothing
but shoes. When I think of African-American rituals
of love, I think not of young, made-up unwed mothers
who seek warmth in the arms of any brother
with arms because they never knew their fathers
(though that could describe my mother), but of that girl
and me in the basement of her father's four story Victorian
making love among the fresh blood and axe
and chicken feathers left after the Thanksgiving slaughter
executed by a 3-D witchdoctor houseguest (his face
was starred by tribal markings) and her ruddy American
poppa while drums drummed upstairs from his hi-fi woofers
because that's the closest I've ever come to anything

remotely ritualistic or African, for that matter.
We were quiet enough to hear their chatter
between the drums and the scraping of their chairs
at the table above us and the footsteps of anyone
approaching the basement door and it made
our business sweeter, though I'll admit I wondered
if I'd be cursed for making love under her father's nose
or if the witchdoctor would sense us and then cast a spell.
I have been cursed, broken hearted, stunned, frightened
and bewildered, but when I consider the African-American
I think not of the tek nines of my generation deployed
by madness or that we were assigned some lousy fate
when God prescribed job titles at the beginning of Time
or that we were too dumb to run the other way
when we saw the wide white sails of the ships
since given the absurd history of the world, everyone
is a descendant of slaves (which makes me wonder
if outrunning your captors is not the real meaning of Race?).
I think of the girl's bark colored, bi-continental nipples
when I consider the African-American.
I think of a string of people connected one to another
and including the two of us there in the basement
linked by a hyphen filled with blood;
linked by a blood filled baton in one great historical relay.

TALK

like a nigger now, my white friend, M, said
after my M.L.K. and Ronald Reagan impersonations,
the two of us alone and shirtless in the locker room,

and if you're thinking my knuckles knocked
a few times against his jaw or my fingers knotted
at his throat, you're wrong because I pretended

I didn't hear him, and when he didn't ask it again,
we slipped into our middle school uniforms
since it was November, the beginning

of basketball season, and jogged out
onto the court to play together
in that vision all Americans wish for

their children, and the point is we slipped
into our uniform harmony, and spit out *Go Team!*,
our hands stacked on and beneath the hands

of our teammates and that was as close
as I have come to passing for one
of the members of The Dream, my white friend

thinking I was so far from that word
that he could say it to me, which I guess
he could since I didn't let him taste the salt

and iron in the blood, I didn't teach him
what it's like to squint through a black eye,
and if I had I wonder if he would have grown

up to be the kind of white man who believes
all blacks are thugs or if he would have learned
to bite his tongue or let his belly be filled

by shame, but more importantly, would I be
the kind of black man who believes silence
is worth more than talk or that it can be

a kind of grace, though I'm not sure
that's the kind of black man I've become,
and in any case, M, wherever you are,

I'd just like to say I heard it, but let it go
because I was afraid to lose our friendship
or afraid we'd lose the game—which we did anyway.

BLACK HISTORY

X wrapped his hands around my throat,
and I wrapped my hands around his,
and then the two of us were in the wet grass

wrestling beneath a star clogged night
like two heads fighting for the same body
or maybe like two bodies fighting

for the same head while a circle of black
and white kids, and the girl who had been
his valentine (and would be again) watched.

This was after the annual Black History Month
Talent Show where my roommate and I sang
"Lift Every Voice and Sing" shirtless and baby-oiled

in black jeans in the name of what I'd call now
Dumb Buck History, but what I thought then
was a way to look sexy for all the girls

in the audience. We lost to two black leather-clad
brothers who recited Run DMC ("Two years ago
a friend of mine asked me to say some MC rhymes . . .")

passing the big mic back and forth between lines,
and I know now it makes sense since
Black Cool seemed worth more than Black Pride,

rap worth more than gospel that day, and anyway
my roommate forgot several of the words
which would have been alright since no one

in the building (myself included) knew
the whole song, but instead of playing it off,
he moaned *Baaaybay, Baaabay* and began to grind

toward the first row and though everyone laughed
(our performance becoming a burlesque comedy
routine) I knew we'd lose, cursed by the ghosts

of Black History Month Decency for going bare backed,
and I was cursed twice, really, (the whole no shirt thing
was my idea in the first place) since X, the jilted lover

of my valentine, was waiting for me in the parking lot
and had in fact been in the audience watching me
defile what probably for him was a very important day

(It was February 14th), and I'm sure he was seeing red
when I too gave up on the Black National Anthem,
and began to gyrate for the audience like my roommate.

/

ROOT

My parents would have had me believe
there was no such thing as race
there in the wild backyard, our knees black
with store-bought grass and dirt,
black as the soil of pastures or of orchards
grown above graves. We clawed free
the stones and filled their beds with soil
and covered the soil with sod
as if we owned the earth.
We worked into the edge of darkness
and rose in the edge of darkness
until everything came from the dirt.
We clawed free the moss and brambles,
the colonies of crab-weed, the thorns
patrolling stems and I liked it then:
the mute duty that tightened my parents'
backs as if they meant to work
the devil from his den. Rock and spore
and scraps of leaf; wild bouquets withered
in bags by the road, cast from the ground
we broke. We scrubbed the patio,
we raked the cross hatch of pine needles,
we soaked the ant-cathedrals in gas.
I found an axe blade beneath an untamed hedge,
its edge too dull to sever vine and half expected
to find a jawbone scabbed with mud,
because no one told me what happened
to the whites who'd owned the house.
No one spoke of the color that curled
around our tools or of the neighbors
who knew our name before we knew theirs.
Sometimes they were almost visible,
clean as fence posts in porch light;

their houses burning with wonder,
their hammocks drunk with wind.
When I dreamed, I dreamed of them
and believed they dreamed of us
and believed we were made of dirt or shadows:
something not held or given, irredeemable, inexact,
all of us asking what it means to be black . . .
I have never wanted another life, but I know the story
of pursuit: the dream of a gate standing open,
a grill and folding chairs, a new yard boxed in light.

I. MJ FAN LETTER

Dear K.O.P., for the first dozen years of my life
I never looked at myself. I believed mirrors
bore no true social significance partly because
they hung on walls. Convinced, then
in the last thin quarter of the century,
that I was a colorless American boy without detail
perhaps I should confess my very first brush with love
involved a white girl and empty dryer box.
I smelled, if I recall, the scent of damp cardboard,
which was a scent not altogether unlike my father's
olive green Army-issue boot socks, and so it was
that as I and my little cob-webbed nymph
(as I have thought of her ever since) attempted
to make a singular glistening smile, I thought again
and again that my father was walking barefoot
nearby with a boot in each fist. I felt
the ominous pre-tingling a soldier feels
when he waits in a trench at the start of a great war
though that was not a year of war, if you recall,
but a year of myriad insignificant misdemeanors
and dumb disputes. I thought too, that the girl
had dropped down into my arms from a nest
of the July, late afternoon darkness blooming
in the upper corner of the box because her hair
danced and dangled across my brown wobbling head
like something made in the belly of a spider,
and I half wondered then when I would learn
what magic it was that gave some creatures the power
to spin a thread almost thinner than light. I decided
I'd ask my father later when I sat on his chest
full of sprawling powder-white women,
and removed his boots and then his socks,
but of course I didn't, having been struck dumb

by *something* (The color or length of his toes,
the tiny grid pattern the socks left on his ankles?).
It doesn't matter what, since any boy who spends
an afternoon with a girl in a box is prone to forget
his questions. I too had a bizarre über-hunger
for companionship and have gone on having it,
as I presume you have, ever since. When I pressed
my palm against the girl's back, I felt first,
the impression of her skin inside the white blouse,
and then the jagged bones of her spine
and I thought of the tiny, tiny spines
in all the animals inside and around the box
when we found it there at the edge of the park.
The stray dogs had spines shaped like my father's
belt, the squirrels and field mice had spines
shaped like the smallest limbs of the saplings;
I thought briefly of grasshopper and ant bodies
before considering the spinelessness of the earth-
worms uncoiling in the mud beneath the box.
Mostly I learned what I know of myself
by holding my tongue still and I'm wondering
how it was with you? Anyone can go back
to the summers that were clear as water,
and I'm assuming you too sat at opened windows
and listened to the world. Perhaps I shouldn't say
yet what it was you and I were waiting for, Cousin,
but I'll say it never arrived.

II. A FEW RUMORS CONCERNING MR. POTATO HEAD

Bet in his diary there are blueprints of his faces. *Yep, and a little arrow pointing to where his eyeball rolled from the page.* Yep, and bounced once on the floor. *Bet a diamond glistens in the ear floating in the mason jar on his desk.* Bet his collar-bone is made of gold. *Bet he's never heard of Mary Shelley*—Hell, bet he can only read sheet music! *Goddamn, Brother, Prince just changed his name!* Doctors say latex is ageless. *Doctors say the body is nothing but money.* Bet his tongue quivers in a pillbox. *Bet his tongue is shy, in debt, and depressed.* Bet he sings: Praise be to Edison's lightbulb and the scalpel! *Bet he sings: Praise be to the nursemaid who sells her womb!* Bet he sings: Praise be to hyperrealism, hypodermics, John Merrick and the poise of mannequins! *Bet it'll be a closed casket in the end.* And enough flowers to cover Texas. *And a dozen biographies in the first month!* Yep, bet no one finds the diary. *Bet no one finds the face.*

III. OMNIPOP, 1982

Little things like pants get a mind of their own. They get their legs and then their waistband and then the pants begin to run in place. Little things like pants extend the song and fill it with mirrors and glitter. The pants shrink and turn to shrieks. Smaller and smaller, the pants shriek and shrink until they can fit inside other pants, until they can fit the legs of a chimp and then the fingers of a hand—the little pants remember childhood and their longing turns them into panting, the sound a doll makes. The world needs miniature pants. Bless the little pants.

IV. RSVP

~~Dear Michael, I have never had to look~~
~~into mirrors. Or rather everything I look into~~
~~(magazines, televisions, sheetrock, shut doors,)~~
~~is a kind of mirror. Everywhere I look~~
~~I see my face. Thank you for sending~~
~~the autographed photograph. And thank you too~~
~~for the sequined glove! Your hand~~
~~must be so small and naked now without it.~~
~~The interior reminds me vaguely of fresh wood,~~
~~or maybe the inside of a cardboard dryer box~~
~~circa 1975, the year I kissed a black boy~~
~~named Clarence or Terrance or Tyrone.~~
~~He was a skinny moth-boy as shy as you.~~
~~Sometimes I wonder what would have happened~~
~~if I'd let that black boy stay inside~~
~~my mouth . . .~~ Dear K.O.P., this is not a letter
from one of the white girls you met
backstage in Columbus or Lincoln, but from me—
your friend, pretending to be a white girl
in the hope that this time you might reply.
Oh, to be in the head of a pretty white girl!
It's nearly impossible even for a black boy
raised late in the era of integrated cafeterias,
Mtv and soap operas. By now your experiment
must be nearing its sad inevitable conclusion.
Are you asking yourself: Am I the beginning
of beauty or am I the end? I'm fairly sure
that's not something white girls ask themselves,
though it's something everyone wonders
about them. Africans, Asians, Martians, Apes—
they love them some white girls and you
have to wonder: is it all the PR (from Helen
of Troy to Mary Christ to your Elizabeth Taylor)?

PS thank you for the egg sized diamonds.
PS thank you for the cashmere panties.
What's the deal with you and Elizabeth?
What's the deal with you and Diana,
the Butch Diva, for that matter?
Once you could have had the love of anyone.
I can still remember your hyper-glow socks
and fly tuxedo. Sometimes my thoughts drift
to Billie Jean, that condemned anonymous woman.
What ever happened to her and that baby?
(Dear Michael, finally the cameras look in
another direction. Our child grows
in a big nosed quiet. He sang to himself
in the womb like you. I tell him
he has a bevy of uncles who once loved
synchronized dancing; who live now
somewhere nose to nose in a crowded mansion.
Baby, I don't believe in music anymore.)
What's a brother got to do to get an answer,
Brother? If by chance, this is the first of my letters
you are reading (I've written dozens
over the years), let me say again
that I understand a man's hunger for company.
When I moved North and phoned home
to tell my momma I'd fallen in love,
she asked me if the girl was white and I snapped,
"No Ma, she looks like you!"
That's got to be one of the most outrageous
(maybe most reasonable) questions,
my mother has ever asked me . . .
"Take love where you find it," "Water is the color
of what holds it," and all that.
What does your mother think of your hair
and lipstick? Of all the girls' noses
pressed at your limo window in 1982,
which did she most adore?

THE BLUE BARAKA

We go waaaaay back, America.
Like mutts in the bed of a pickup.
Like righteous indignations.
Like riotous ignitions. Like far right-
wing indicators blinking
white&black, white&black, white&black—
They don't share our values, you say.
I gave you my life / you gave me
my life, America. Some of us fog
up the grapes and some of us vomit
money. Some of us bag boys. Some of us
Lerois, some of us Charlie too Browns
too. Some of us black-eyed, brown-
eyed idlers. Some of us be best friends
or fried fiends, but all of us be
floundering interiors, be all these things
at once, America. Why you be?
Why you be decked in suits
of metal? Indefatigable. Empty
fat. Inflatable. Laughable and lost.
Why you be funkying up the holy waters
and memorizing the same Biblical bullshit?
He shall separate us one from the other,
as a shepherd divideth his sheep, you say.
He shall divideth the chain from the gang,
divideth the pepper from the pepper-spray,
you say. You say: *They don't share*
our values. America, how you talk
with such little lips? How you sleep
with such little rhythm?
How you live with such little music?
You be your own ship at sea.
You be your own shadow off course,

the last hour, the shroud of transgressions.
You be a white, blue and ready-made utopia
for some; you be over-cooked
and crooked, a scythe of bite marks,
an odor of orders for others.

THE BLUE BORGES

Pessadilla, Ephialtes, Incubus, Alp,
Black Horse, a blind man cannot see
the night. I dream the moon
and I dream my eyes perceiving
the moon. When I dream of Buenos Aires,
my father is talking up and talking down
the genius of Gustav Spiller
with coffee and a cockatoo. Scharlach
was the name of a German schoolgirl
and Escarlata the name of her twin
in Madrid. Macedonio Fernandez,
Alfonso Reyes, Maria Kodama, Rafael
Cansinos-Assens, Don Nicano Paredes,
the caudillo of Palermo—*El amor
o el diálogo de unos pocos.* I wanted to lie down
with each of them and run with each of them
in a fresh meadow the way a river lies down
and runs in a meadow. I wanted to be shelter
and fire like that builder of the Great Wall
and burner of all the books written before him,
the first Emperor, Shih Huang Ti,
who outlawed all the words for death
and paid his sorcerers good money
to invent the elixir of unlimited health;
the screwball Shih Huang Ti,
who called himself the first Huang Ti
so as to be in some way the original
Huang Ti as he wandered a palace
that contained as many rooms as there are days
in the year. Decay loves the ramparts,
the stairwells, the terraces, the parapets,
the galleries, the patios, the cloisters,
the cisterns, the chambers, the anterooms,

the dungeons, the vaults. Decay loves the cells.
Decay loves the inscriptions. Decay loves
decay and neither I nor the executioners
of the State can do anything against this love
because it is a love that does not decay.
"Alles Nahe werde fern," said Goethe,
but it is also true that everything distant
becomes near. *The Intellectual Voyage*
of Paul Groussac; the beloved blue
Boethius who worked the toll booth
between Free Will and Providence;
An Experiment with Time by Dunne;
Dante waits with Virgil in my father's study.
A line by Verlaine that I have forgotten;
Guatemala, Serrano, Paraguay, Gurruchaga;
Juan Diaz de Solis who rowed upstream
in 1516 to be consumed by Indians;
Hipolito Irigoyen, the twice elected,
couped Argentinean president; terraqueous
daguerreotypes wait in that circular room
with walls and doors that are mirrors.
I remember the phony infinitude of the self.
I worship the dream of the yellow tiger
which can only be hunted by men
riding the back of a Persian elephant.
Pessadilla, Ephialtes, Incubus, Alp,
Black Horse, I want to lie down in darkness
and dream of the fresh meadows
that have vanished, and the rivers
that have also vanished. I long as Spinoza said
all things long in their being to persist.

THE BLUE BOWIE

This guy wept
and told us
he wanted to touch
the earth
with the fury
of a falling star.
This guy wore snow-
storm glitter and bangles
of lightning and tears
back when our slogan was:
Never Pull A Slow Gun
lest your children's link
with you be broken
and they janitor
a blank banner of surrender
into and out of
all the iridescent cities
of War.
All modern thought
is permeated by the idea
of thinking the unthinkable.
Ziggy Stardust,
Ziggy Stardust,
A moonage daydream, Baby,
put your ray gun to my head.
Black as a black hole,
why does your big electric pupil
keep looking at me?
I could write my name
in the makeup
on your face.
Sweet blue boy
with a black wind

whistling
through the spaces
between your teeth,
O, whoa, whoa, whoa,
you're a rock n roll suicide.
The song has gone
on forever
And you say, as it is said
Samuel Beckett said
at the end of his life:
What a hell of a morning it's been . . .

THE BLUE ETHERIDGE

Dear Parole Board of the Perennial Now,
let me begin by saying it's very likely
none of my ex-wives will vouch for me.
Let's just say the parable
of the Negro who uses his dick for a cane
and the parable of the Negro who uses his cane
for a dick convey the same message to me.
I'm sorry. You mean before that?
Well, it's as if some ghost the height
of my granddaddy was lighting a cigarette
the wrong way to symbolize my muddy path
through life. You ever seen the Mississippi?
You'll learn all you need to know
if you look at the wall of my kinfolk's pictures.
Belzora. BuShie. My sisters. Me
and my brothers fishing in high waters.
Whenever I see brown hills and red gullies,
I remember what the world was like
before I twisted spoons over flames.
I pissed from a bridge the day I left.
Yes Sir, I've changed, I've changed.
But I won't be telling you the story
of the forlorn Negro or the Negro cutthroat
or the Negro Hero or the Negro Tom.
I won't be telling you the story of the night
I died. I believe everything comes back
to music or money. Belly Song.
Song of the twelve-fingered fix.
Song of The Gemini Women. I know I'm cursed.
I sang out to the Baptists I saw gathered
on the riverbank the day I left. I sang out
to the reeds straight as tongues and the salmon
in the waters of my people, and beyond that
to my barrel-backed shadow damming the stream.

HARRYETTE MULLEN LECTURE ON THE AMERICAN DREAM

Mud is thicker than what is thicker than water. Pull your head up by your chin straps. Put the pedal to the metal. Peddle to the middle. Put the medal on the pedestal. I pledge Sister Sledgehammer & Father knows beds, but I am not my breather's keeper. I pledge to earn every holler & if found guilty, I pledge to repay my Bill of Rights to Society. From me to shining me. Money, money, money, monkey. We're number none. Our number's done. *E Pluribus Unum*bskull. For war & several fears we go. Praise be to Guard. Slops & slobbers. Maladies & Gentrifications. Don't kill us, we'll kill you. With lobotomy & Jesus for all.

ORACLE

What was it you wanted to know? Television is very good and useless if you have no memory. I was going to say there will be no end to the rift between you and your mother. But then acceptance is a fine, fine name for defeat. A closet filled with shoeboxes with no shoes? Has she done a lot of walking away? And Pops tap-dancing on the remote? The greatest mystery to Man is Man and the universal beauty of Clint Eastwood's face. On the Animal Channel, an Asiatic Black Bear adheres to a pear tree. How close are you willing to get, if it means getting eaten? What kinds of weapons do astronauts take into space? Look, the world is everywhere: satellites, end tables, the pink and white poinsettias outside the church; reunions and degrees. All those radiant asterisks . . . Soon it will all make sense.

MAUSOLEUM

Well, let's get right to it: my parents live in a mausoleum. It's never too late for someone to kill someone else. No obit says of the recently dead: "He was cruel, he was low down and selfish, the world is brighter without him," but wouldn't that be great? In October: the leaves, the leave-taking. Here, you will not be getting something for nothing. It is not all new or available for a limited time only. Here, one gets more things to get more things. When the blood exits, it does not return. And one day maybe you find a box of your mother's poems in the basement. Wouldn't that be great? And to do nothing! To grow huge and short-breathed like a mantle of what-nots. Like the elderly. Like a childless couple with three cars. Like a house with a television in every room.

IT'S A SMALL WORLD

They look at you, you look at them, they look at me, I look at you, you look at me, we look at them a few billion times. The world? I realize there's nothing else like it: someone someone knows always somewhere unexpected, infinite varieties of bad poems and plant life. Inanimate subjects, subliminal as line breaks. One thing follows another. Me? I know sirens are especially bad news when they come for you. I know you can trade money for anything but money, but have you seen those flat screen digital televisions that cost more than a gold plated crack pipe? (I was going to say *There will always be laughter,* but then I'd have to explain.) I crawled out dumb as a rock and webbed like you. Wedded to catchphrases and conspiring factors. Mortal and fairly ugly sometimes, though sometimes not. But lately, Friend, when you and I are together, I feel more solitude than I do alone.

UPRIGHT BLUES

I. New Orleans Piano Genius

He knows the name of every street
in Vaudeville.
      A brown boy's legs
bend on the steps
of a red house like his fingers
      on slats of light
& black keys. A thumbnail-
moon rests
      on the flag. A crocodile
pulls out of the swamp:
suitcase of fire-
      water & a train-
ticket to Birdland.
      One of Ringo's
henchmen will unscrew his eye.
From the wig of a live oak,
      a star will shake free.
The anthem of New Orleans.
Napoleon's sword
on a backdrop of blue feathers.
      Stalks of sugar cane.
Pride black
as a preacher's robe.
      He is ready to sing
Sweet Chariot
in his father's company.
White gloves,
      the hands
covered wagons moving
into the valley.
      Hump-backed,

crooked-letter vein.
     He knows
sometimes evil can ransom
a good man.
          He knows the name
of every street in Vaudeville.
His fingers
          rest on the knob
of the door to a red house.
& the black star tattooed
on the white boy's waist,
          the flesh
of a halved moon opens
          his mouth,
his fingers on slats of light,
          black keys.

II. Gonzo's Blue Dream

When these knuckles climbed
the keyboard's edge to the moon,

they were my blues. I had a little song
for the departing day. I was a stray

rooster-throated, bellowing hole.
I was a slim penny-colored skin.

A bank of two-sided wounds
in phenomenal light. I had a little song

for the departing night. I transformed
& was transformed by pleasure.

I was damn near invisible
like ice cubes fading into light.

Friends, I want you
to never have a song for death.

Once in the arms of a stranger
at the hour the paperboy wakes,

I asked God to give me a different life.

III. Papa Was a Rascal
"You know my papa was a preacher, & a lover too . . ."

Mister Scripture, Mister 6ft,
Patent leather shoe.
Cuff-link, velvet robe,

& the booze
& the singed fingers,
Why can't I be a rascal too?

Your Cadillac,
Your jubilant chorus,
Your ribs of polished pews.

& the strand of hair,
Soft as a silk rose,
& the stains

Of a milked moon
On the legs of your suit.
I want to be a rascal too.

The Lord's prayer,
The tray of withered dollars,
The organ-holler,

The field moan
Of a young man
Who will find Jesus,

& before reaching home,
Lose him again.
I want to be a rascal too.

Father, take this music
Spilling out of my fingers.
Take my wrist watch,

& house keys
& patent leather shoes.
Take my left eye

& puncture me
With needles,
Leave me in the junkies' ward.

Mister Pulpit,
Mister Culprit,
Mister Wine,

No one in Heaven or Hell
Will ever stop loving you,
Papa, why can't I be a rascal too?

IV. Booker's Tomb

Airline Highway.
Sheetrock houses hurricanes

can turn to mud,
the trees in ruffled sleeves,

the smell of winter
covered in rain.

No songs are called
from bones. In the cemetery

Time has hushed
the medley of the blood.

That luscious afro wig,
that eye patch & flowing cape

are gone. To find you
James Booker, I have gone

into the palace of the dream.
I have gone to the bar

where the piano player
could not play your song.

I have gone to the bar
where the dope dealers

still look for you,
I have sipped water

on the couch
in your sister's house

while the mantel of photos
called your name:

Maharajah. Liberace. Little flame
beneath a spoon. The scent

of peeled moonlight
tunneling to the brain.

James Booker I have come
here to find you. How long

will I be whispering your name?

THE BLUE KOOL

Yo, you soft as the flesh beneath my thumb
nails. That's why I cut you. I'm

that third rail, that live wire.
Yeah, I'm that PI for hire,
that Dark Age, serf-made spire.

You need to say your prayers.
You need to believe your naysayers.

Those parachute pants you wear
are baffling. There's hot air

in your bread basket. You penny-loafer.
I got a chauffeur.

I'm laughing. Your tour bus
behind my limousine, Boy, you can't pass

it. I'm too cool. I freeze the wannabees,
I melt the moon, I hand my butler my top hat, I tease

my afro with my afro pick. My head is on
right. I'm fur collared, cashmere, double down,

diamond-button trench coat.
You goodwill jacket.

You anti-hazardous.
You crack to my Angel Dust.
Better run before you get your butt

kicked. You plastic spastic.
You manic matchstick.
I'm hot like that sunlight and Classic

Rock. I'm that Black Elvis, that Black Bach,
I'm too cool. I grind my pelvis, my back

crack, your mamma back crack too.
I give her love bites. I'm daddy to you.

Brush your teeth, empty your bladder
before you greet me. That fat
girl call you *Honey,* all her kids call you *Daddy,*

the bastards. You have my sympathy,
but you can't have my money.
Don't write no symphonies

or rap songs about me.
Your style is lousy.
Yeah, Boy, I'm too cool. Don't talk about me.

THE BLUE MELVIN

The choir said to me: *Sweetback,*
what happened to the sun?
Nigga this, Nigga that,
then more Hallelujahs,
God's gonna trouble the water.
There wasn't all the *de rigueur*
you see nowadays.
This was when there were no protests
outside the Blues & Spirituals,
because no one believed words
were more important than music.
All the maverick Negroes
were eating croissants
in the Bye & Bye by then.
Broke my heart.
I must have run
all the way to Galilee chanting
They won't bleed me. Won't bleed me
Trouble ain't no place to be!
I woke up in Paris
with a kazoo for a grin.
I kept my Cable-car
Conductor's card though.
This little light of mine.
I'm gonna let it shine,
you know that one?
I wanted to say more
so when I came back Stateside
I started singing
what the Germans call *sprechstimme.*
I invented rap.
I discovered *Earth, Wind & Fire.*
The choir sang "Stormy Weather"

and I decided there would be no scene
in which something is broken
& after which everything is changed.
I was plenty black
& deep down dirty dog scared.
Half Panther, half panhandler.
I dreamed I was on a ship
& woke up on a ship.
But if God's gonna trouble the water,
what I care about a little rain?

THE BLUE SEUSS

Blacks in one box
Blacks in two box
Blacks on
Blacks stacked in boxes stacked on boxes
Blacks in boxes stacked on shores
Blacks in boxes stacked on boats in darkness
Blacks in boxes do not float
Blacks in boxes count their losses
Blacks on boat docks
Blacks on auction
Blacks on wagons
Blacks with masters in the houses
Blacks with bosses in the fields
Blacks in helmets toting rifles
Blacks in Harlem toting banjoes boots and quilts
Blacks on foot
Blacks on buses
Blacks on backwood hardwood stages singing blues
Blacks on Broadway singing too
Blacks can Charleston
Blacks can foxtrot
Blacks can bebop
Blacks can moonwalk
Blacks can beatbox
Blacks can run fast too
Blacks on
Blacks and
Blacks on knees and
Blacks on couches
Blacks on *Good Times*
Blacks on *Roots*
Blacks on *Cosby*

Blacks in voting booths are
Blacks in boxes
Blacks beside
Blacks in rows of houses are
Blacks in boxes too

THE BLUE STROM

Never let the ink
of biographers touch you,
but if it happens
learn what you can
of their witchcraft.
It will be useful
should you ever find yourself
without linen.
I would never have risen
above backwoods,
bow-tied Superintendent
or circuit judge had I not studied
the alchemy of metaphor.
There are maybe two dozen gaps
in a given sentence.
Never mistake silence
for death or obedience.
Just because an anthem can't be heard
over the bluegrass
of lawn parties and amphitheaters
doesn't mean it can't be sung.
If you stand on the porch
of the state house on a Sunday
you will hear the great flag
of the confederacy.
On some occasions
you may have to lower an earlobe
to the tongue whipping in the mouth
of the one Negro servant
who remains when everything else
is burned. Avoid anyone,
even your secretary, who talks
openly about revenge.

Master the filibuster,
for it will wear out the sentries
of heaven. Cultivate horticulture.
Marry after forty. Outlaw basketball.
Outlaw school buses. Outlaw
the manufacturing of transistors.
Outlaw jive-talk and rhythm.
If you intend to be re-elected
certain moods must be abolished,
it goes without saying. Remember
your duty. If you must apologize,
let it be in a language no one comprehends.

PINE

I still had two friends, but they were trees.

—*Larry Levis*

In the dark we lugged someone's farfetched bounty
From a truck's black cab and it was a bad idea
And a bedevilment better than the rocks we'd thrown

At the dogs behind each low fence, the branches we'd torn
From saplings barely rooted to the fields, Boomie and I,
Our heads in a swivel of trouble, our two tongues

Swigging distractions, a few hour's worth of wrong turns
Behind us, we were restless and miles from home,
Dark boys roaming in the dark. We found a pickup truck

Unlocked outside a small hotel and in its cab: trash bags
Fat with clothing and housewares, a toaster and vacuum,
Waiting to be used again by someone checked in for the night,

Maybe a runaway wife reversing her dreams, a streak
Of red wine sleeping on her tongue while elsewhere
Her husband was in the dark because he didn't know yet:

She was gone, she was gone. For no good reason
We took the bags from the truck and propped them
Below the pine trees which like everything in the dark,

Belonged to us. And to anyone approaching, our laughter
Must have sounded like the laughter of crows, those birds
That leave everything beneath them trampled and broken open,

Those birds dark enough to bury themselves in the dark.
But we were not crows, and we were not quiet until it was too late.
I was thrown against a tree as if I weighed less than a shadow,

A hand clutched the back of my neck as if it wasn't a neck.
Cuffed later inside the break-proof glass, I watched
The policemen nuzzling everything we'd touched,

Slithering, their faces calculating absolutes while the trash bags
Shimmered in a fiasco of light. When I looked up,
I saw Boomie nearly twenty feet high in the arms of a pine,

Almost nothing visible, but his white shirt and white shorts.
I could feel him feeling as sorry for me as I felt for him,
And I said nothing. Think of what the tree might have said

If it could speak: *Hold me for a moment then, let me go . . .*
Something an unhappy housewife might say
To her husband on the last night of their marriage,

Or a boy to policemen when he's locked in a squad car.
I heard a voice between their voices issuing numbers,
Codes or uninterpretable verses, addresses in a bewildered city.

I was to be taken somewhere and given a name
More bona fide and afflicted, I was to be shot
Through the knee and then shot through the jaw,

Boomie must have thought. Even when the scene was clear,
He must have remained. It must have been like clinging
To the massive leg of God—

If the leg of God is covered in bark, if prayer is like waiting
For the darkness beneath you to change into something else,
If it's like waiting in the darkness to be changed.

A GIRL IN THE WOODS

Why wouldn't she have wanted to be there at first,
riding low into whatever song the radio played,
that girl running her nails along the worn backseat

of a Cadillac, beat-up and beach blue
with a busted muffler and fur-covered steering wheel,
that car clamorous and big enough to seem ridiculous

rambling from the high school parking lot
with laughter in its belly: two thin brown boys upfront
and the thin brown girl they'd promised a ride home

rocking in the rearview, music coating their teeth?
She might have wanted to be there because
they were her friends, just as they were mine,

and when their long blue door swung open,
even you might have climbed in and gone smiling
behind their tight-lipped tinted windows,

and you would have had nothing to fear
until they turned from the road and parked in the woods,
as they turned and parked that day where the road was soft:

the brown boys who turned to reach for the brown girl
and coo how she was about to be raped.
They should have known better than to fool around that way.

I remember the way your mother told me to take off
my sneakers and wait for you in the hallway
before our first date, and the sound of her footsteps following

you through a room somewhere in that house
as she warned you against staying out late with a boy like me.
After we'd parked and made love kneeling in the woods,

I laughed and asked you why she had to be that way.
I have thought of your body in the underbrush for years.
And I have thought of the story you told me about being raped.

Because they were my friends, they told me the story
they had promised to never tell: how the girl wept
even after they raised their naked palms, promising

it would be okay. It was a prank, it was a simple mistake.
They should have known better than to fool around that way,
those boys who were not boys, men who were not men,

their narrow veins, narrow rivers
of hunger branching into muscle and skin.
Who made the road leading from the road?

What was the song they sang before turning off?
Who made them stop? Maybe her weeping
made them become themselves again,

or made them something they had not been.
Before they reached her house, each of them trembling,
I imagine the girl drying her face, her mother looking

from the window when they pulled into the driveway.

THRESHOLD

No steps remained, but we did not leap
from the knee-high grass of that house
abandoned in the woods to the porch

with the planks that were as loose and warped
as those of a small boat beached long ago
by someone who rowed one last time

from a lake in a kind of reverse drowning,
the kind that calls one permanently to land
when someone has been lost, the water opening

indifferently and closing in the same manner
until even the oar strokes were traceless,
the boat left to become more and more

vaguely like the ribs of something that lived once,
that had purpose, but now could not hold a body,
could cradle nothing except the occasional rain

and wind the way the body cradles breath—
the warped, narrow wood of the porch
reached beyond us, me and the daughter of a man

who had been like me, who had been young
when this house was new and warmed by people
we would not ever know except by way of a black sock

someone had used to wipe away shit or semen
and left in the corner before going out again
to the porch and yard to sink

into the will of whatever else makes up the woods.
Seeing the sock then told me some of the possible history
of the world around us: that others had come here,

probably the girl's older brother had been hiding here
while their father knocked at almost every door
in our neighborhood looking for him one night,

and maybe the cool somber-jawed dropouts
had been here, and other couples
who could not afford hotels,

others had left crushed and uncrushed cans
and clouded bottles, stick porn and mottoes
and aliases on the walls; they'd left their smell there too

and the roof seemed to want to guard it
though when the windows were smashed,
the doors kicked open, some of their musk

had been swept into the woods where it met the two of us
approaching with nothing but our caution
and green irrevocable hunger, and we could see it

would not hold us, the old porch,
so we did not leap from the knee high grass
to get in, we stepped as lightly as others had crossing

planks that splintered and cried out
as if to the old house and maybe to the deep, deep woods
and to the path others had not intended to leave.

THE WHALE
for Purvis

Just like that your father's dead,
Half of all the footsteps you've made

In your lifetime swept away by the tide
Gnawing the shore, the bits of shells
Like fragments of bone and teeth sinking

Into the sand beneath you as you walk
Toward the people crowding the body

Of a young whale, a boy on the shoulders
Of his father, a woman slipping film into a camera,
The skin peeling on a lifeguard's neck

As he stoops peering into the animal's eye,
Saying nothing, the audience silent or silenced

By the sound of saltwater sweet-talking the shore
As if sweet-talking the earth from her prom dress,
The tide stroking its hands along her inner thigh

And finding the crop of razor bumps
Like the humped tiny backs of shells

And smiling at the thought of the girl preparing
For her prom date, the hair lathered
And shaved away, the air leaving ripples inside

The dress as the knee-high hem is lifted
Above the girl's waist and breasts,

The sound of the silk passing over her body
Like the sound of the tide uncovering
And then covering the hard news of the day,

The news returning each time it's washed away.

VARIATION ON A BLACK CINEMA TREASURE: BROKEN EARTH

Broken Earth
Year of Release: 1939
Running Time: 11 minutes
Cast: Clarence Muse and unidentified boy

I am the sick boy in the shack when the camera opens
On the sunrise and wispy silhouettes of the plow
And the fool mule and my father working a row down

The middle of a rock field with a small shack in one corner
And a shade tree in the other where a crew of barefoot

Old black men stoop and sing "All God's Chillun Wear Shoes"
And call out *Hey* and *Hi* and the name of my father
Who goes on plowing into sundown, into the dark hour

When the mule will grunt no farther and the red eyes
Of the black men's cigarettes blaze and flicker in one corner

Of the field as I quiver in a wet skin in the hot small light
Of the lantern blazing and flickering in the shack.
I am a sick boy. I am as still as a kettle of water. I am waiting

To be rearranged by the hand of God, which is not the hand
Of God, but the strip of cloth pressed against my brow

By my father who has no medicine but prayer.
I don't know what I did to get here mumbling
"Pappy" and calling out to the ghost of my mother

As a choir sings "Swing Low, Sweet Chariot" somewhere.
I don't know who it is telling me to open my eyes.

VARIATION ON A BLACK CINEMA TREASURE:
BOOGIE WOOGIE BLUES

Boogie Woogie Blues
Year of Release: 1948
Running Time: 10 minutes
Cast: vocalist and pianist Hadda Brooks performing three songs

If you have slept in a house made of nothing but a smile
That drooped around your neck like a five pound chain;
If you have whittled all the virtuous words in the Bible down

To *Amen* the way pillow talk can be whittled down to a tongue,
You know the name of my song: "Don't Take Your Love from Me."

Don't take your love away from me. Your house key.
Your toothbrush. Your swing and sweet scripture
Of touching and preacher's breath. Don't take your fingertips

And hunger from my ears. I know the lyrics
Of the oldest love song: "Don't You Think I Ought to Know."

Don't you think I ought to know, Baby, the doctrine of the Blues,
The spells and fevers of the Blues, the Blues' epistemologies?
I know the lyrics of the oldest love songs. And the new ones too.

Why bother rise and dress now that you are gone?
Why bother boogie woogie? "I'm Tired of Everything but You."

TOUR DAUFUSKIE

On that small island
during a tropical storm
in the last century

people tied to the necks
of pine trees drowned

when the wires and whips
and webs and ropes
of rain covered their bodies

so that when we moved
along the dirt back roads
and paused

to photo the AME church
and one room schoolhouse
and small shacks
of the black folk of Daufuskie

no voices trailed us
or floated out to greet us.

Sometimes now
the trunk of a tree
resembles the waist
of a black body;

sometimes your naked waist
still and rooted before me,
smells thick and sweet
as the freshly cut meat of a pine.

When I knock against you,
it is like swimming from the world

out to the small island of Daufuskie
in the witching hour of a storm,
like drowning in the arms of a tree.

A POSTCARD FROM OKEMAH

Turned from the camera's eye, hovering,
between river & bridge, the hung woman
looks downstream, & snagged in the air
beside her, the body of her young son.

They are tassels on a drawn curtain;
they are the closed eyes of the black boy
who will find them while leading his cow
to the river bank; they are the bells

that will clamor around the animal's neck
when it lowers its head to drink.
The boy dangles in midair
like a hooked fish, his pants hanging

from his ankles like a tail fin.
On the bridge women pose
in aprons & feathered bonnets,
the men wear wide-brimmed hats

with bow ties or dungarees;
there are three small girls leaning
against the railing, & a boy nestled
beneath the wing of his father's arm.

I count sixty-seven citizens & children
staring at what must have been a flash
& huff of smoke. The photographer
must have stood on a boat deck,

though from this angle
he could have been standing on the water
with his arms outstretched.
He must have asked them to smile

at the camera & later, scrawled his copyright
& condolences on the back of the postcards
he made for the murdered man's friends.
"The Negroes got what would have been due

to them under process of the law,"
the sheriff said. His deputy
had been shot when the posse searched
the suspects' cabin for stolen meat.

To protect her son, the mother
claimed she'd fired the gun.
The mob dragged them both
from the jail bound in saddle string.

If you look closely you can see a pattern
of tiny flowers printed on her dress;
you can see an onlooker's hand opened
as if he's just released a dark bouquet.

Now all of Okemah, Oklahoma, is hushed.
Now even the children in attendance are dead.
After that day in 1911, it did not rain again.
To believe in God, this is the reckoning I claim.

It is a Monday morning years too late.
All the rocking chairs & shopping carts,
all the mailboxes & choir pews are empty.
I cannot hear the psalms of salvation

or forgiveness, the gospel of Mercy.
I cannot ask who is left more disfigured:
the ones who are beaten or the ones who beat;
the ones who are hung or the ones who hang.

THE BLUE TERRANCE

I loved Bruce Lee and a ten dollar ukulele.
For my little mutt Shepherd and the saplings,
I performed black Superman melodramas barefoot
on the picnic table until a toenail opened
on my big toe like the hood of my father's Lincoln
and a fever broke. I dropped stuff.
I showed Erica (my queen) McQueen
my junior penis. I showed Connie Simpson,
I showed Meko Jackson, I showed Precious Jones,
and again and again they split like pigtails
on a trampoline. (I wanted to possess
and be possessed.) I was not allowed
to make eggs and rice or lasagna.
"Blood!" my gang said. "Blood, blood, blood!"
until someone fainted. We were *The Booty Snatchers*
until a fifth grader slapped Ronnie.
We were *The Hell Cats* until Sammy & *The Big Dawgs*
jumped the fence. We were *The Dream Team*
until we awakened. There was a boy
who could win at H-O-R-S-E on crutches.
There was a girl in a black training bra
and a mother in silk pajamas. That was the year
Baybay held me out a window by my ankles.
I began an obsessive regimen of drawing
Peanuts. (Charlie Brown began with an O.)
I was not allowed to take showers.
There was a deep inarticulate grief
for David Banner and a high frothing euphoria
for the Hulk. There was a law
that said sooner or later you'll hear the rivers
of the skull, the small islands
where volcanoes erupt. (I waited to erupt.)
I kept my head up to keep the blood off

my sneakers. I feared roaches more than divorce.
My muscles weighed less than my skin.
My neighbor, Mr. Black Belt, nearly broke my wrist
before he vanished. Let's just say all those knuckle-
sandwiches taught me mercy. If you can remember
the dreams where your mouth is full of mulch,
you can imagine the tongue in a granny knot,
a train wreck of a sentence jammed inside a throat,
a gullet piping steam, the air inside a fist.

THE BLUE TERRANCE

I come from a long line hollowed out on a dry night,
the first son in a line of someone else's children,
afraid of water, closets, other people's weapons,
hunger and stupidity, afraid of the elderly and the new dead,
bodies tanned by lightning, afraid of dogs without ethos,
each white fang on the long walk home. I believe all the stories
of who I was: a hardback book, a tent behind the house
of a grandmother who was not my grandmother, the smell of beer,
which is a smell like sweat. They say I climbed to the roof
with a box of lightbulbs beneath my arm. Before the bricks,
there were trees, before the trees, there were lovers
barely rooted to the field, but let's not talk about them,
it makes me blue. I come from boys throwing rocks
bigger than their fists at the head of the burned girl,
her white legs webbed as lace on a doily. In someone's garage
there was a flashlight on two dogs pinched in heat.
And later, a few of the puppies born dead and too small
to be missed. I come from howls sent up all night and all day,
summers below the hoop and board nailed to a pine tree.
I come from lightbulbs glowing with no light and no expressions,
thrown as far as the will allows like a night chore, like a god
changing his mind; from the light broken on the black road
leading to my mother. Tell me what you remember of her
now that her walk is old, now that the bone in her hip strains
to heal its fracture? I come from the hot season
gathering its things and leaving. I come from the dirt road
leading to the paved one. I will not return to the earth
as if I had never been born. I will not wait to become a bird
dark enough to bury itself in midair. I wake up sometimes
in the middle of the country with fur on my neck.
Where did they bury my dog after she hung herself,
and into the roots of what tree are those bones entangled?

I come blessed like a river of black rock, like a long secret,
and the kind of kindness like a door that is closed
but not locked. Yesterday I was nothing but a road
heading in four directions. When I threatened to run away
my mother said she would take me wherever I wanted to go.

THE BLUE TERRANCE

If you subtract the minor losses,
you can return to your childhood too:
the blackboard chalked with crosses,

the math teacher's toe ring. You
can be the black boy not even the buck-
toothed girls took a liking to:

this match box, these bones in their funk
machine, this thumb worn smooth
as the belly of a shovel. Thump. Thump.

Thump. Everything I hold takes root.
I remember what the world was like before
I heard the tide humping the shore smooth,

and the lyrics asking: *How long has your door
been closed?* I remember a garter belt wrung
like a snake around a thigh in the shadows

of a wedding gown before it was flung
out into the bluest part of the night.
Suppose you were nothing but a song

in a busted speaker? Suppose you had to wipe
sweat from the brow of a righteous woman,
but all you owned was a dirty rag? That's why

the blues will never go out of fashion:
their half rotten aroma, their bloodshot octaves of
consequence; that's why when they call, Boy, you're in

trouble. Especially if you love as I love
falling to the earth. Especially if you're a little bit
high strung and a little bit gutted balloon. I love

watching the sky regret nothing but its
self, though only my lover knows it to be so,
and only after watching me sit

and stare off past Heaven. I love the word *No*
for its prudence, but I love the romantic
who submits finally to sex in a burning row-

house more. That's why nothing's more romantic
than working your teeth through
the muscle. Nothing's more romantic

than the way good love can take leave of you.
That's why I'm so doggone lonesome, Baby,
yes, I'm lonesome and I'm blue.

A SMALL NOVEL

The protagonist spends the first twenty pages
crossing a bridge wearing nothing but red
swimming trunks and sneakers with no socks.

I can remember standing naked
outside my neighbor's window at fourteen
when I read the paragraph about the placard of night

held up by pine trees.
Wherever there is a mention of solitude or desire
I think, without wanting to, of Race. Race

when the protagonist spends a page long sentence
trying to work free a knot of shoe string
in his basketball sneaker. Race

when he spends the hot seasons of his twenties
like a beggar with no mouth. Race
when he tells his wife: *"There are no Open Houses*

on Easter." Late in the book he feels himself
becoming a shadow. On page 113 just as I reach
the final sentence about traffic like the sound of wind

like the sound of water, a horn yelps somewhere.
"It was all he'd ever known of rivers . . ."
I pencil L.H. in the margin. I think, without wanting to,

That they will find this book someday
and turn its muddy bosom all golden in the sunset.
On its blank last page I write the poem

"The Blue Langston" which begins:
"O Blood of the River songs, O songs of the River of Blood,"
and ends: "There was nothing I could do about Race."

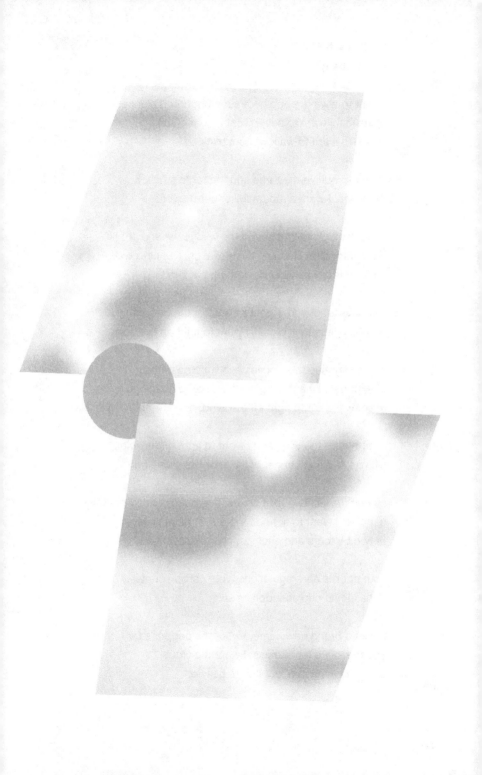

WIND IN A BOX
—after Lorca

I want to always sleep beneath a bright red blanket
of leaves. I want to never wear a coat of ice.
I want to learn to walk without blinking.

I want to outlive the turtle and the turtle's father,
the stone. I want a mouth full of permissions

and a pink glistening bud. If the wildflower and ant hill
can return after sleeping each season, I want to walk
out of this house wearing nothing but wind.

I want to greet you, I want to wait for the bus with you
weighing less than a chill. I want to fight off the bolts

of gray lighting the alcoves and winding paths
of your hair. I want to fight off the damp nudgings
of snow. I want to fight off the wind.

I want to be the wind and I want to fight off the wind
with its sagging banner of isolation, its swinging

screen doors, its gilded boxes, and neatly folded pamphlets
of noise. I want to fight off the dull straight lines
of two by fours and endings, your disapprovals,

your doubts and regulations, your carbon copies.
If the locust can abandon its suit,

I want a brand new name. I want the pepper's fury
and the salt's tenderness. I want the virtue
of the evening rain, but not its gossip.

I want the moon's intuition, but not its questions.
I want the malice of nothing on earth. I want to enter

every room in a strange electrified city
and find you there. I want your lips around the bell of flesh

at the bottom of my ear. I want to be the mirror,
but not the nightstand. I do not want to be the light switch.
I do not want to be the yellow photograph

or book of poems. When I leave this body, Woman,
I want to be pure flame. I want to be your song.

WIND IN A BOX

If so, let me go on into the imaginary city.
At first, how cool it would be
to recite a dozen prayers as a last name.

Or as no last name at all. Words passed
to me by strangers. Let me enter
with a pre-assembled strut.

If my life amounts to a fence
between two dogs,
who wouldn't want to disappear?

If it amounts to a lover's teeth prints,
let me sleep a night or two in that city.
In the beginning was the couple burning

in the dark. See how that could go on
forever? If the imaginary city is cut through
by rivers, the idea makes me want bridges.

If it is lockless, let there be no thieves,
let there be no bad luck. Damn right.
If I am less than smoke to my mother,

the African-American, and less than smoke
to my father, the bull, so be it.
I know life is spent between two chasms.

Half buttoned. Nostalgia, the bread
by which we live. Say this:
"Half boy-funk, half emptiness."

The only beauty curved towards my heart.
I turned my back to whatever divine yammering
filled me. I don't call it the past, but I call it

something as predictable and far reaching.
Someone was waiting to be born.
And you're right, someone was guilty.

WIND IN A BOX

Even the dirt dreams of it now.
It is two roads along two rivers,
The sky above a mother's face

The day her husband leaves
For war. No blood and stars
But the blood and stars.

Let's find it and break its fucking neck,
Let's break its fucking jaw.
Let's break its fucking ganged in vessels

And if it pushes back and a tiny blue rises
On its cheek, let's break that too
Until stars dance in the corners

Of its eyes like white seeds
And let's break those too
Until all the words we know are split in two.

No power but the power of need.
Let's get up ready to feel.

God bless the rage in us.
It's how we know each other.
We who keep vigil by the windows,

We who pour ashes from the windows
Into the wind, skin passing over skin.
Let's walk up the hill and along the rows

That do not ask questions.
Near the white and yellow flowers,
Strangers are moored in sighs.

Soon it will rise without kissing
Anyone goodbye.
It says we will not be renewed,

We will not be filled
Like the birdhouse.
It says we will arrive unwashed.

Aren't you tired? Let's lie down.
Let's cry out and rest.

WIND IN A BOX

I claim in the last hour of this known hysterical breathing,
that I have nothing to give but a signature of wind,
my type-written handwriting reconfiguring the past.

To the boy with no news of my bound and bountiful kin,
I offer twelve loaves of bread. Governed by hunger,
he wanted only not to want. What is the future

beyond a premonition? What is the past
beyond desire? To my brother, I leave a new suit, a tie
made of silk and shoes with unscuffed bottoms.

To the mirror, water; to the water, a book with no pages,
the author's young face printed on the spine.
I wanted children taller than any man on earth.

If everyone was like me, I said to the mirror.
To my lover, I leave enough stories to fill an evening.
Enough sleep to walk from one coast to another

without pause. I held no counsel with God.
I cut open the fruit of a tree without speaking to the tree.
I ate food prepared by strangers. To the black cashier,

I leave nothing. Her story is like the one I was given.
To all the carpenters looking at the ceiling, nothing.
Here in the last moments of my illiterate future,

may the people know I did not matter.
Shoeprints at the door. Shoeprints on the old road.
To the boy with two lights going on and off in his stare,

I leave the riddle of the turtle who had shelter,
but no company. To the black girl, grace. To the black girl,
mirrors; a father blessed with the gift of mind-reading,

men who do not wound her, men she does not wound
herself for, and mother love. Unable to shed the old skin
and stand, I stand here in the hour of my hours alive.

These words want to answer your questions.
These words want to stave off your suffering,
but cannot. I leave them to you. Enough sky

and a trail. Wood and enough metal for machines.
Tell me, what am I going to do when I'm dead?
Let my shadow linger against the earth, protect my children.

IMAGINARY POEMS FOR THE OLD-FASHIONED FUTURE

1. Sooner or later I'm going to have to talk about the white house and how the men there don't seem to like big butt women.

2. There will also be a praise poem for the smartest, strongest, and/or fastest human alive should he or she live in a region with no reporters, printing presses, indoor plumbing etc.

3. And further additional efforts to demonstrate the ways my mind transforms day to day happenings into stuff. (parts 1–30)

4. A poem by someone named Lester Sea. Someone named Lenore. Headline sonnets maybe. Titles ripped from the annals of jazz bebop, no doubt.

5. Written in seat 9A between Chicago and Traverse City. Little shacks with stoves on the big iced lake. (Fish cakes in the stoves.)

6. An "I love big" button somewhere. ("I love you, Portly, don't let 'em take me . . .")

7. Part I: "Viscous Circus," Part II: "Victory Circle," Part III: "Vicious Service," and if there's a Part IV: "Very Surly."

8. "Dwell," "Furl," maybe. Girlish laughter in the pipes. (Keep talking, we know the same people.)

9. "The Short Age" followed by "The Us Age" followed by "The Bond Age" followed by "The Volt (or Re-volt) Age" followed by "Dose Ages," "Mile Ages," and "Out Ages." (See journal appendix.)

10. Definitions of *Divine Imaging, Speed Lightning,* and *German-tic Racial Demography.* (Pronunciations of *logistic* as *lowget-stick; stroll* as *scroll*)

11. Half a dozen one hundred line attempts at resolving the poem: "I come from a long line of . . ."

12. A tercet rhyming bric-a-brac, brick a black, and poppa bag.

EVERYBODY GOES TO HEAVEN

The deceivers, each of them wringing their undersized hands, and the unrepentant wearing snow shoes that leave question marks on the dirt road behind them; the insomniac gang from the ninth circle; the crew of bloodshot despots, the dictators rubbing their rope burns; a Judas for each hour of eternity—they all show up when the news gets out: everybody goes to Heaven. The doorman sees them coming and scratches the bald spot behind his ear, his mind drifting towards the next gig now that his job is done. The saints and zealots who had no lives beyond duty, the ones who whispered into the ears of folk like my parents, the converts, the most blind and love-struck: they will spend their retirement painting sublime landscapes and portraits of their persecutors. A pair of bristle-jawed lynch men find their victims and invite them to lunch at a restaurant made of mist. The wrong-doers with no bodies settle into the no bodies of the wronged. Phrases like *I'll pray for you* and *God Bless you* or *be with you* become obsolete. No one need step out into the wide blue night looking down and looking back and looking up. No one need bother looking for the Truth. The vote outlawing Church passes nine to one. The preachers form a Lonely Hearts Club, and meet week nights in tents outside town. The theologian finds the book God had been reading by the pool, but finds no God. Some of the minor sinners, the superfluous, the revelers of part time desire, remain in the post office waiting for word.

And what becomes of the righteous, the ones who lived lives full of absolute faith and virtue? They picket, mope or pace outside the open gates. You can imagine their outrage. Their version of Heaven has become a ring of smoke. It has become a thing of the past, and the past has become all that's left. They are so full of the past, they cannot be changed now. They are so full of Heaven, they cannot be filled.

IT CAN'T BE GOOD SITTING AROUND IMAGINING
YOUR DEATH

Anyhow, leave the World Book Encyclopedias to the book peddler
who will never travel beyond the poor black college kids peddling
    their history
books at semester's end. It might be the grass growing
on the plots of dirt above our ancestors that makes me say this.

It might be the white woman or man our son or daughter will marry
and the white woman or man our grandson or granddaughter will
    marry,
all of them wading into the future until one of our line claims to be
    Sicilian.
Leave instructions: the granddaughter of our granddaughter shall be
    named Cicily.

If all men are created equal, all men are prophets,
at least at the very start and end of their lives, I bet.
Cicily, as the curse I'm casting here prescribes, won't like blacks
any more than she likes looking into a mirror in a burning house.

Still, I can almost promise you time travel will never be invented.
At first Cicily will think someone rescued our photograph
from a puddle of ashes. It's like those stories
we wind up telling ourselves about ourselves after our friends are
    gone.

It's as if we will always be somewhere smiling or singing.
Maybe you can imagine the end of the line, Baby, but history
is beyond me, I admit it. Either she will discover my apology
or she will never be forgiven, and that will be a function of the curse.

It's like one of those days that are wished for, but never guaranteed.
She will marry a man who says: "But blacks *are* different, they were
    burned
black by God." "They dance in their sleep." "I love you" will slither
from its little sheath of hunger and that too will be a function of the
    curse.

Which is why not too long ago you and I argued about race
and the question was: If I don't believe in evil, do I also not believe in
    good?
I meant to say yes, because my mother loved me as if one of us was
    two people.
Remember when our three year old asked why we weren't white?

To be black is to blacken a little every day, I should have said.
And how at the end of a life filled with music we all go without singing.

THE HERITAGE CHANNEL

In the movie about the making of the movie about slaves
a dust colored chandelier was hanging
like a dust covered chandelier in the foyer
of an abandoned mansion and my pout-mouthed Ma
said she wanted to find a chandelier like that—
she'd get one of the homeless to hang it for a six pack
and transportation she said, and who said anything about slaves?

We spent a few nights smudged between the walls.
Nights of inviolate wine and laughter, mornings with a finch opera
       outside our windows.

I come from a long line of hairdressers in wigs,
of blind folk in shades: a caught line, a long line
of bastards and farmers with no sons, of jibber jabber,
of "I'll put my foot so far up your ass, you'll be shitting my footsteps,"
of "she used to," "he used to," and "we," and ennui,
of "When was that?" and "Who?" and "That's why they call it work."

We spent a few nights in the village.
Nights trading subservient curtseys
below a ceiling fan hanging like a chandelier.

There I was shoveling a furry former body into the trunk
and phony to say what were the eyes were lit
as if my headlights still cooked each pupil and that look
rimmed in stupidity could have easily been mistaken for peacefulness
were it in the face of a dead man and it was.
Who said anything about slaves?

A few nights tethered together.
A few nights attending our own show.

I come from a long line of bastards. My mother remembers
a black man who arrived one Sunday.
Her sister and two brothers called him Stranger.
They said "Your daddy brought you nothing," jealous,
when she went with him across town to see his distant cousins
who sat on the porch of a fine blue house asking
"How is your wife?" "How is your daughter?" "Who is that child?"

Saying the blood is burgundy after dark.
Saying the dark is blood.

Say *Evil* and the word will drain your good sense,
but sing it and the child will know her father ran away or was run over
and buried all the same. It might win you Providence
should you have the sort of know how the Lord is said to possess.
That's why they call it Faith.

Muzzled in cool wind.
Muzzled in moonshine and deaf as a placenta.

I come from a long line of dead men.
My grandfather's medals rust in a felt lined case,
kept safe and forgotten by a daughter
who has his name but only half his blood.
The houseplants reaching for the dirt,
the night's color seeping through holes
left by the pictures she took from the walls.

There is no such thing as evil without love.
No one asked about our wardrobe.
We talked to, but not with.

That damn fool was in the woods asking for moonshine
when, like a spill of black ants exiting a corpse,

the Negroes of the American South crawled North
to the small and various catacombs of industry.
My kinfolk stayed behind with him trying on names
the way one tries on shoes at a sharecropper's funeral.
Who said anything about slaves?

A few nights attending our own movie.
A few nights muzzled in booze.

They said "Your daddy brought you nothing,"
when she returned, her shoes shined by the cuff
of his white, white sleeve, her breath sweet with candy
that traveled all the way from New Jersey in his pocket.

We returned so covered in history,
we had to wash it from our scalps.
I opened the window and I was not to be trusted.

I come from a long line of divas who taught themselves
the wrong love and were too generous with it,
too made-up and covered and dancing
at happy hour with lips the color of wine.

We spent a few nights smudged between the walls.
Nights with the finch opera outside our windows.

Thirty years later she looked into his coffin like someone looking
into water and smelled flowers pulled from the bank of a river,
grease in hair brushed flat, shoe polish, her twin half-sister
ringed in pearls and white silk, half the life she'd dreamed of at her
    back.

We spent a few nights in the village.
Nights of inviolate beer and laughter.

Behind us waiting below the oak tree or on the red hoof-trampled
   road
beyond the tree or further, in a house beneath a tin roof
the wind whistled through, a girl prayed
so intently for a dress that the prayer lingered in the blood
she passed on to her daughter and her daughter on to me.
Who said anything about slaves.

Muzzled in cool wind.
A few nights tethered together.

I would have believed history was beyond me,
had I no black suit and no umbrella
and had the carpet along the aisles not been so thick
my feet never touched the floor
and were Ma not saying *Good God,*
Good God and dabbing money at her eyes.
That's why they call it Blood.

WIND IN A BOX

In one of those parallel worlds that race

at each ear of the universe a boy and father rise

at sunrise to lead you away. You risk

the same things there you risk

here. The scar buckled to your wrist

there is here. But maybe you do not wish

for the same things there as here. Wash

your bones of their narrative. It was

not always as it is. (Could be it was worse.)

Some of the locks are covered in rust

there. The boy's axe blade curves like the rind

of an ear. From there maybe you ride

a current here. The wrongs done there, you right

here. And the wrongs done here, you right.

NOTES

"The Blue Borges" is based predominantly on lines and details in Jorge Luis Borges's *Selected Poems* (Penguin, 1999) and his essays in *Everything and Nothing* (New Directions, 1999). The Spanish line in the poem translates: "The love or the conversation of a few friends"; the German line translates: "Everything near becomes distant." "The Blue Bowie" is inspired by lyrics from *The Rise and Fall of Ziggy Stardust and the Spiders from Mars.* "All modern thought is permeated by the idea of thinking the unthinkable" is a quote from Michel Foucault. "The Blue Etheridge" makes reference to Etheridge Knight's poem "The Idea of Ancestry." "The Blue Kool" is inspired by the rapper Kool Keith. "The Blue Melvin" is inspired by liner notes and lyrics from the CD *The Melvin Van Peebles Collection* (Stax, 1999). The "Upright Blues" sequence is dedicated to James Carroll Booker, the late great New Orleans pianist. The "Variations on a Black Cinema Treasure" poems are based on two film synopses from *Black Cinema Treasures: Lost and Found* by G. William Jones (University of North Texas Press, 1991). "A Postcard from Okemah" is based on a photograph in *Without Sanctuary: Lynching Photography in America* (Twin Palm Publishers, 2000).

Photo by W. T. Pfefferle

ABOUT THE AUTHOR

Terrance Hayes is the author of *Hip Logic* (Penguin, 2002) and *Muscular Music* (Carnegie Mellon University Press, 2005; Tia Chucha Press, 1999). His honors include a Whiting Writers Award, the Kate Tufts Discovery Award, a National Poetry Series award, a Pushcart Prize, a Best American Poetry selection, and a National Endowment for the Arts Fellowship. He teaches in the English Department at Carnegie Mellon University and lives in Pittsburgh, Pennsylvania, with his family.

PENGUIN POETS

JOHN ASHBERY
Selected Poems
Self-Portrait in a Convex
 Mirror

TED BERRIGAN
The Sonnets

PHILIP BOOTH
Lifelines: Selected Poems
 1950–1999

JIM CARROLL
Fear of Dreaming: The
 Selected Poems
Living at the Movies
Void of Course

BARBARA CULLY
Desire Reclining

ALISON HAWTHORNE
 DEMING
Genius Loci

CARL DENNIS
New and Selected Poems
 1974–2004
Practical Gods
Ranking the Wishes

DIANE DI PRIMA
Loba

STUART DISCHELL
Dig Safe

STEPHEN DOBYNS
Mystery, So Long
Pallbearers Envying the One
 Who Rides
The Porcupine's Kisses
Velocities: New and Selected
 Poems: 1966–1992

ROGER FANNING
Homesick

AMY GERSTLER
Crown of Weeds
Ghost Girl
Medicine
Nerve Storm

EUGENE GLORIA
Drivers at the Short-Time
 Motel

DEBORA GREGER
Desert Fathers, Uranium
 Daughters
God
Western Art

TERRANCE HAYES
Hip Logic

ROBERT HUNTER
Sentinel and Other Poems

BARBARA JORDAN
Trace Elements

MARY KARR
Viper Rum

WILLIAM KECKLER
Sanskrit of the Body

JACK KEROUAC
Book of Blues
Book of Haikus

JOANNE KYGER
As Ever: Selected Poems

ANN LAUTERBACH
Hum
If in Time: Selected Poems,
 1975–2000
On a Stair

CORINNE LEE
PYX

PHYLLIS LEVIN
Mercury

WILLIAM LOGAN
Macbeth in Venice
Night Battle
Vain Empires
The Whispering Gallery

MICHAEL MCCLURE
Huge Dreams: San Francisco
 and Beat Poems

DAVID MELTZER
David's Copy: The Selected
 Poems of David Meltzer

CAROL MUSKE
An Octave Above Thunder
Red Trousseau

ALICE NOTLEY
The Descent of Alette
Disobedience
Mysteries of Small
 Houses

LAWRENCE RAAB
The Probable World
Visible Signs: New and
 Selected Poems

PATTIANN ROGERS
Generations

LEE ANN RORIPAUGH
Beyond Heart Mountain

STEPHANIE STRICKLAND
V: WaveSon.nets/Losing
 L'una

ANNE WALDMAN
Kill or Cure
Marriage: A Sentence
Structure of the World
 Compared to a
 Bubble

JAMES WELCH
Riding the Earthboy 40

PHILIP WHALEN
Overtime: Selected Poems

SUSAN WOOD
Asunder

ROBERT WRIGLEY
Lives of the Animals
Reign of Snakes

MARK YAKICH
Unrelated Individuals Forming
 a Group Waiting to Cross

JOHN YAU
Borrowed Love Poems